METAMORPHIC, IGNEOUS AND SEDIMENTARY ROCKS

SORTING THEM OUT

GEOLOGY FOR KIDS

Children's Earth Sciences Books

BABY PROFESSOR

EDUCATION KIDS

Speedy Publishing LLC
40 E. Main St. #1156
Newark, DE 19711
www.speedypublishing.com

What are the different kinds of rocks? How do they form? Where do you find them? Read on and find out!

Folded limestone on Crete, Greece

OUR ROCKY WORLD

Rocks are made of minerals. They form in different ways on and in our Earth's crust. The three main types of rocks each form in different ways. The three types are:

- **IGNEOUS ROCKS** formed by molten rock that cools, either on the surface of the Earth or far inside our planet.

- **SEDIMENTARY ROCKS** that form from tiny fragments of material that make layers that build up over time on the Earth's surface.

- **METAMORPHIC ROCKS** that form under extreme temperature and pressure in the Earth from igneous or sedimentary rocks.

Together, rocks make up the lithosphere, the outer layer of the Earth. The lithosphere is about 100 kilometers thick.

Concepts in Geology

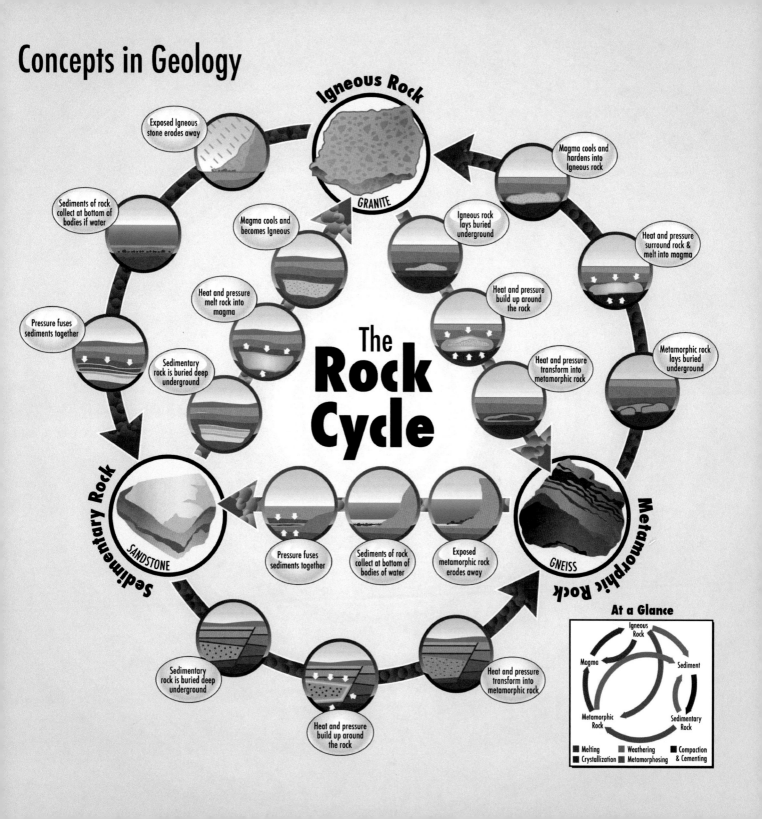

Igneous rock cliffs at Queen's Bath in Bahamas.

IGNEOUS ROCK

Igneous rocks form from molten rock, or magma, which cools and crystallizes into minerals. Geologists use the size and composition of the crystals to classify the rocks.

They are generally the hardest and densest of all rocks, although pumice can be so lightweight that it floats on water. When a volcano erupts very violently, the rock it throws into the atmosphere can develop many tiny air pockets that makes it light.

The way igneous rocks look can depend on the composition of the magma they formed from and the rate at which they cooled. Magma that cools quickly has small crystals, except for obsidian, which has no structure of crystals. Basalt has small crystals you can only see using a microscope. When magma cools slowly it creates rock like granite, with large crystals that have had time to develop.

Close-up of various igneous rocks.

Magma cools slowly when it is inside the Earth's surface, creating plutonic rocks. When it cools quickly on the surface of the Earth, it creates volcanic rocks. Plutonic rocks are also called intrusive igneous rocks and the other term for volcanic rocks is extrusive igneous rocks.

Basaltic lava flow in Hawaii.

MANY TYPES OF IGNEOUS ROCKS

Magma can be made of different mixes of chemicals and gases, and form at different temperatures. The differences in magma can lead to the creation of different rocks. There are more than 700 types of igneous rocks! Here are some of the most common types:

- Andesite
- Basalt
- Gabbro
- Diorite

- Peridotite
- Obsidian
- Scoria
- Tuff

Obsidian

Sedimentary rock/Cemented sand dunes created by the processes of entrainment, transportation and deposition on land, by wind.

SEDIMENTARY ROCK

All sedimentary rocks were once sediment, tiny fragments of other rocks and other material that were broken down by erosion, wind action, rocks grinding together, and other natural processes. The sediment may be carried by water a long distance before it settles, or may form layers not far from its source. However, water is often the vehicle that carries sediment along to where it will eventually become part of a rock formation. About seventy percent of the *"Skin"* of our planet is made of sedimentary rock.

There are two main ways sedimentary rocks form on the surface of the earth.

CLASTIC MATERIAL

Clastic material is pieces of hard material, including flakes of bones and pieces of other rocks. They become cemented together, through a combination of chemical action and evaporation of water, until they form sedimentary rocks. They can form in or under liquid water, in deserts, or because of the action of glaciers.

Collection of specimens of various sandstone rocks.

SEDIMENTARY MATERIAL

Sedimentary material is layers and layers of small fragments, which might be from other rocks or organic material like limestone, that gradually cements together.

CLASSIFYING SEDIMENTARY ROCKS

It's tricky to classify sedimentary rocks, because differences in the chemical composition of the rock material, the process of sedimentation, and whether organic material is involved can result in very different types of rock.

Collection of specimens of limestone rock.

In general, these are the standard classifications:

- **CLASTIC ROCKS.** These are collections of fragments of other rocks that have been carried by water, lava flow, or other materials until they come to rest in layers. There are different types of clastic rocks depending on the crystals they contain. These are usually crystals of quarts, mica, clay, and feldspar.

- **CONGLOMERATES.** Conglomerates have a large proportion of rounded gravel.

Set of sedimentary rock specimens - Shale, Conglomerate, Argillite, Mudstone, Travertine, Limestone, Tufa, Arenite, Sandstone, Coquina, Bauxite, Marl, Dolomite, Coal, Flint and Anhydrite.

- **BRECCIAS.** Breccias are like conglomerates, but their gravel has more sharp edges.

- **SANDSTONES.** Sandstone is rock made from grains of minerals and rock that are about the size of grains of sand on a beach. Quartz is the most common mineral in sandstone, and the most common mineral on the surface of the Earth in general.

Isolated sample of a Breccia rock.

- **MUDROCKS.** Mudrocks are made of mud that has solidified. The particles are very fine, and were probably carried by fast-moving water until the speed of the water slowed and the particles could settle.

Collection of specimens of mud minerals.

- **BIOCHEMICAL ROCKS.** Limestone is a biochemical rock, because it is made up mostly of skeletons! Limestone comes from fragments of the skeletons of ancient coral, molluscs, and other aquatic creatures. Coal, formed from ancient trees and other planets under pressure in the Earth, is another type of biochemical rock. Another very interesting type of biochemical rock is fossils of bones of dinosaurs and other ancient creatures!

Collection of specimens of various coal minerals.

Set of various argillite minerals.

- **CHEMICAL ROCKS.** Some rocks are formed by the evaporation of water, leaving a hardened chemical structure behind. Gypsum and Halite (salt) are examples of chemical rocks.

Some common sedimentary rocks include:

- Argilite
- Breccia
- Chalk
- Chert
- Coal
- Dolomite
- Limestone
- Gypsum
- Mudstone
- Shale

Metamorphic rocks layers. Muckross Head, Donegal, Ireland.

METAMORPHIC ROCK

Metamorphic rocks start as igneous or sedimentary rocks. Then, under extreme pressure and high temperature in the Earth, they change. The temperatures are not high enough to melt the rock, or it would form igneous rock. The pressure is much higher than what you need to just break the rock. The pressure and temperature combine to change the chemical structure of the rock.

Different combinations of pressure and heat working on the same rock can result in very different types of metamorphic rocks. For example, if you start with shale, a sedimentary rock, and apply a certain combination of heat and pressure, the result may be slate, which is dense, smooth and does not have visible crystals. Adding more pressure and heat to the slate can generate schist, which has visible layers. Apply even higher temperature and pressure to the schist and you may get gneiss, which has visible mineral bands.

Set of metamorphic rock specimens - Amphibolite, Migmatite, Quartzite, Skarn, Quartz, Schist, Listvenite, Jaspillite, Shale, Coal, Serpentinite, Hornfels, Slate, Phyllite, Gneiss and Talc.

METAMORPHOSIS

Metamorphosis is a Greek word meaning "*Change*", and that's what has happened. Sedimentary or igneous rocks have changed under pressure and heat into something very different from what they started out as. Metamorphic rocks can form under the Earth's surface, or in the turmoil of a volcanic eruption.

Chip metamorphic rock with a layered texture.

The metamorphosis of rocks can happen in two ways:

- **CONTACT METAMORPHISM**
  The other name for this is *Termic Metamorphism.* In contact metamorphism, magma below the Earth's surface is so close to the rocks that the rocks partially melt and start changing their chemical properties. They may recrystallize, fuse crystals, or experience a range of chemical reactions brought on by the extreme heat of the magma.

Layered rock formation folds on the Mediterranean island Crete, Greece.

- **REGIONAL METAMORPHISM**
This also has another name: *Dynamic Metamorphism.* Regional metamorphism happens when rocks deep underground experience extreme pressure. The pressure is so strong that the rocks are sort of squished out and lose a lot of their original features. Heat can also play a part, but pressure is the main thing.

Collection of various actinolite in Amphibolite mineral stones.

Metamorphic rocks can have crystal structures and inherit minerals from the rocks they came from, and they can also have new minerals that are generated by the heat and pressure they experience during metamorphosis.

Blue kyanite, brown biotite, pink tourmaline crystals in druse of gneiss mineral stone.

When you find minerals like *Garnet, Chlorite,* or *Kyanite* in a rock formation, it's a good sign you are looking at (or standing on) metamorphic rock.

Chemical changes during metamorphosis can cause:

- **MECHANICAL DISLOCATION.** This is when the rock, or some minerals within it, become physically changed by pressure.

Hornfels stone.

- **CHEMICAL RECRYSTALIZATION.** When extreme pressure, combined with extreme heat, work on unstable crystals, they can change into other crystals.

Metamorphic rocks are usually divided into two general types:

- **FOLIATED METAMORPHIC ROCKS.** The crystals in these rocks have been squeezed and lengthened under pressure and they generally show some sort of pattern or alignment.

Migmatite stone.

- **NON-FOLIATED METAMORPHIC ROCKS.** These rocks show no particular crystal pattern. Sometimes this is because the material, like limestone, is made of minerals that do not elongate.

Metamorphic rocks can form because of high temperature, high pressure, or a combination of both. The movement of the Earth's tectonic plates creates immense pressure where two plates collide, and this can generate metamorphic rock.

Collection of specimens of serpentine and serpentinite minerals.

Another source of metamorphic rock is volcanic eruptions, when the magma rising through the volcano meets the rock that makes the Earth's crust.

Common metamorphic rocks include:

- Amphibolite

- Schist, which has subtypes like micaschist and blueshist

- Gneiss

- Hornfels

- Marble

- Migmatite

- Phyllite

- Quartzite

- Serpentinite

- Slate

A WORLD OF WONDERS

This Earth is full of surprises, from rocks, to water, to the atmosphere around us. Read other Baby Professor books, like *Peeling the Earth Like an Onion*, *A Giant Shield, and You* and *I Need Water to Survive*, to learn even more about our planet Earth.

Visit

BABY PROFESSOR
EDUCATION KIDS

www.BabyProfessorBooks.com

to download Free Baby Professor eBooks
and view our catalog of new and exciting
Children's Books

Made in the USA
Monee, IL
09 October 2020